A Star Is Not a Planet

and Other Mix-ups in Space

Melvin Berger

Illustrated by Craig Attebery

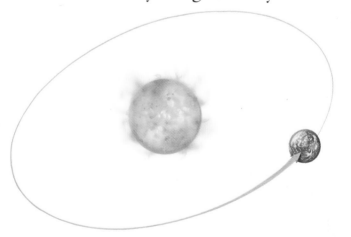

SCHOLASTIC INC.

NEW YORK TORONTO LONDON AUCKLAND SYDNEY

ISBN 0-590-95608-6

12 11 10 9 8 7 6 5 4 3 2 1   8 9/9 0 1 2 3/0

Printed in the U.S.A.   23
First Scholastic printing, March 1998

Contents

A Star Is Not a Planet

A star is a large body in space. So is a planet. But—

Stars are huge . . .

Most stars are many times bigger than planets. The sun, for example, is a midsize star. Yet it is about 100 times bigger from side to side than planet Earth. In fact, about one million planets the size of Earth could fit inside the sun!

Earth

Venus

Mercury

. . . Planets are much smaller.

Jupiter is the biggest planet in our solar system. But
Jupiter is only one-tenth the size of the sun. And Pluto, the
smallest planet, is just 1/600th as big as the sun.

Pluto

Neptune

Uranus

Saturn

Mars

Jupiter

Stars are giant balls of gas . . .

Stars are mostly made up of two gases—hydrogen and helium. The force of gravity holds the gases together in the shape of a ball.

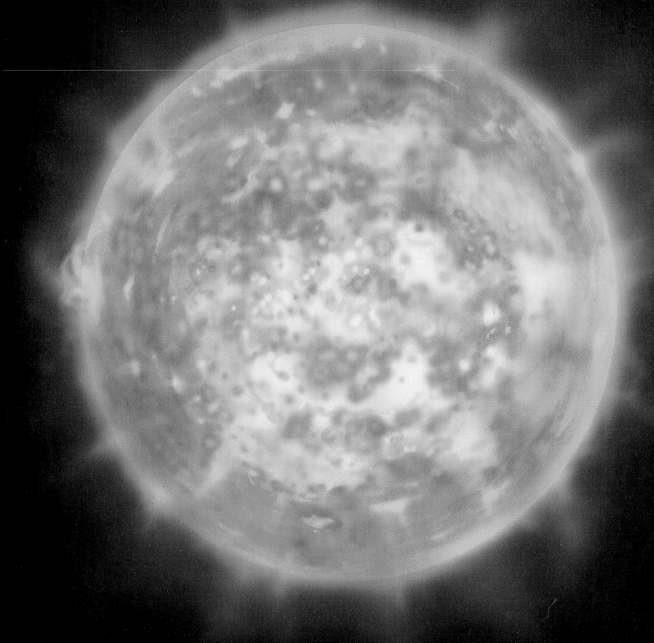

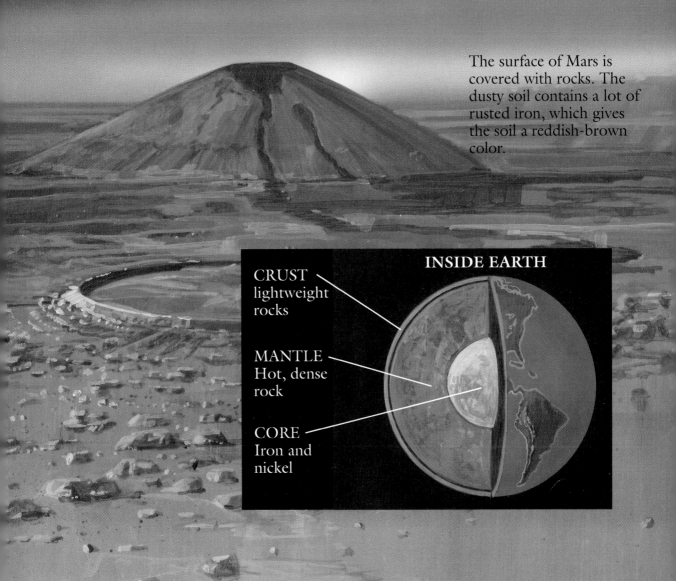

. . . Planets are mostly solid.

The four planets closest to the sun—Mercury, Venus, Earth, and Mars—are made up of rock. Astronomers believe they have metal in their central cores. The next four planets— Jupiter, Saturn, Uranus, and Neptune—also have metal cores. But their cores are surrounded by gas, ice, and liquid. Pluto, the most distant planet, is thought to be all ice.

The surface of Mars is covered with rocks. The dusty soil contains a lot of rusted iron, which gives the soil a reddish-brown color.

INSIDE EARTH

CRUST
lightweight
rocks

MANTLE
Hot, dense
rock

CORE
Iron and
nickel

Stars are hot and bright . . .

Gravity pulls very hard on the hydrogen atoms inside the giant stars. The pressure forces the atoms to join together. This produces immense amounts of heat and light.

We can feel the sun's heat and see its light. But the other stars are much, much farther out in space. We cannot feel their heat. And we can see their light only as tiny points in the sky at night.

Stars twinkle . . .

The light from distant stars comes to us from billions of miles out in space. Each of these stars looks like a little dot. But as the starlight nears Earth it passes through layers of moving air. The shifting air makes the tiny points of light shake and twinkle.

The stars shine day and night. But we just see them at night. During the day, the sun's light blots out the light from the other stars.

. . . Planets are cold and dark.

Most of the planets in our solar system give off little heat
and no light. They get almost all of their energy—light and
heat—from our nearest star, the sun. Only Jupiter and Saturn
produce any real amount of heat of their own.

. . . Planets have a steady light.

The planets are much closer to us than the stars. From
Earth, the planets look more like disks than like dots. But
their light also passes through the moving layers of air
around Earth. This makes the planets look fuzzy—not
twinkly.

Stars seem fixed in space . . .

Stars are always speeding through space. Yet night after night they seem to stay in one place. That is because they are so far away. Only very careful measurements over many years show us that the stars really do move.

We can see about one million stars . . .

Through a telescope, we can see about a million stars in the night sky. Photographs taken through large telescopes show even more stars—around 800 million! And astronomers believe there are hundreds of billions more.

. . . Planets seem to be moving.

Planets also speed through space. But we can see their movement because they are so much closer to Earth than the stars. The ancient Greeks saw these disks moving among the stars. They called the moving disks planets. The word means "wanderer" in Greek.

. . . We can see only nine planets.

Everyone knows that nine planets circle the sun. But are they the only planets in the universe? Not at all! It's just that the other stars are so far away—and their planets are so small—that we can't see them through our telescopes. Astronomers guess that a good number of stars have planets around them—just like our sun!

Revolve Is Not the Same as Rotate

Planets move in two ways: They revolve and they rotate.
But—

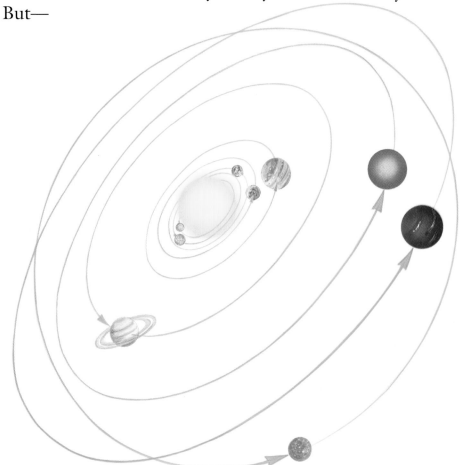

To revolve is to move in an orbit . . .

All planets move—or revolve—along gigantic paths
around the sun. These paths are called orbits. The planets
all move in the same direction. The orbits are oval—or
elliptical—in shape.

. . . To rotate is to spin around.

Each planet also spins like a top—or rotates—as it revolves around the sun. The planet rotates around an imaginary line through its center. This line is called the planet's axis. The earth's axis runs from the North Pole to the South Pole.

To revolve around the sun takes a year . . .

The time it takes a planet to revolve once around the sun is a year on that planet. The length of the year varies. It depends on the planet's distance from the sun and its speed. Mercury is closest to the sun and the fastest. A year on Mercury lasts 88 days. Earth is the third planet from the sun. As you know, a year on Earth is 365 days. Pluto—the farthest planet from the sun and the slowest—takes almost 91,000 days to complete a revolution!

Earth takes 365 days to go once around the sun.

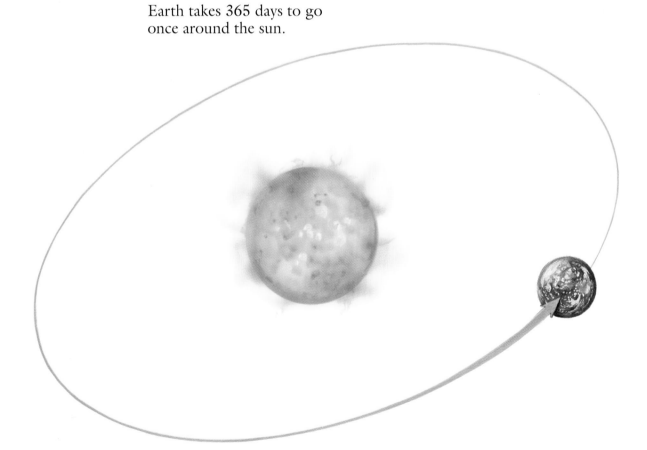

. . . To rotate around an axis takes a day.

A day is the time it takes a planet to rotate once around itself. Each planet has a different length day. A day on Earth is 24 hours. A day on Jupiter is less than 10 hours — the shortest of all the planets. The longest days are on Venus. One day on Venus lasts as long as 243 days on Earth!

A Year and a Day in Space

Planet	Revolving time (year)	Rotating time (day)
Mercury	88 Earth days	59 Earth days
Venus	$7\frac{1}{2}$ Earth months	243 Earth days
Earth	365 Earth days	24 Earth hours
Mars	23 Earth months	$24\frac{1}{2}$ Earth hours
Jupiter	12 Earth years	10 Earth hours
Saturn	$29\frac{1}{2}$ Earth years	$10\frac{1}{4}$ Earth hours
Uranus	84 Earth years	17 Earth hours
Neptune	165 Earth years	18 Earth hours
Pluto	250 Earth years	7 Earth days

Planets revolve at varying speeds . . .

Each planet follows an elliptical orbit around the sun. Part of the time, the planet is closer to the sun; part of the time it is farther away. When the planet is closer to the sun, it moves more quickly. When the planet is farther from the sun, it moves more slowly.

Earth's revolving speed is faster when its orbit takes it closer to the sun.

. . . Planets rotate at steady speeds.

Each planet's speed of rotation stays about the same. Its distance from the sun has nothing to do with its rotation. Nor does a planet's size affect how fast it spins.

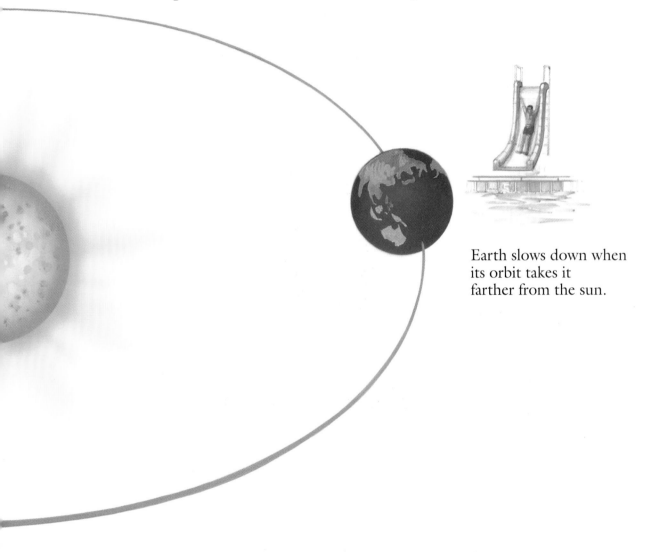

Earth slows down when its orbit takes it farther from the sun.

Revolving speeds are very fast . . .

All planets revolve very quickly in space. But the planets closer to the sun move faster than those that are far away. Mercury, the closest planet, whizzes around at 107,000 miles an hour! The most distant, Pluto, moves only about one-tenth as fast as Mercury. Even so, Pluto zips along at an amazing 10,800 miles an hour!

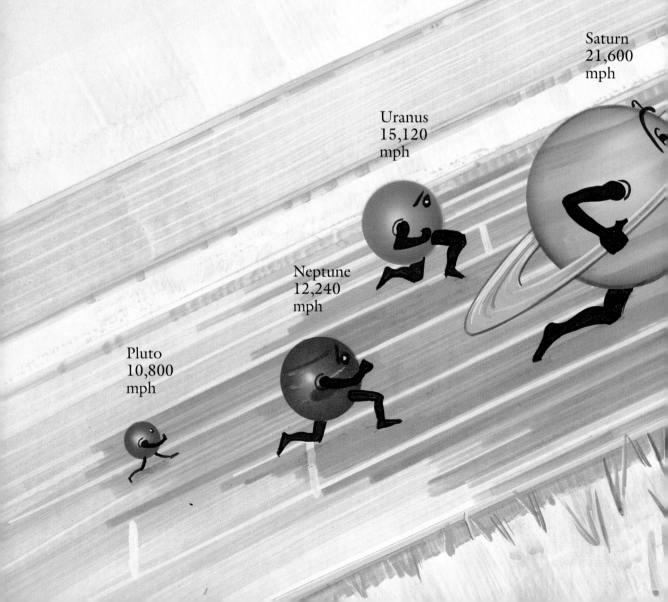

Saturn
21,600
mph

Uranus
15,120
mph

Neptune
12,240
mph

Pluto
10,800
mph

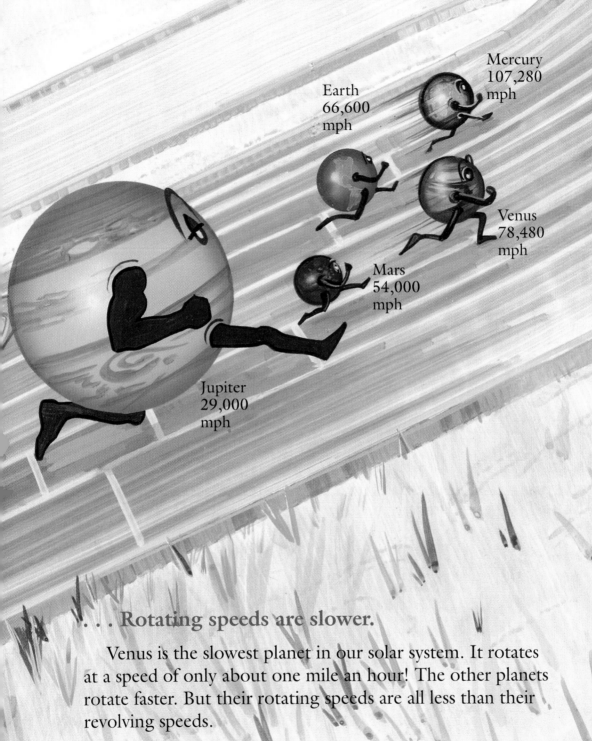

Mercury
107,280
mph

Earth
66,600
mph

Venus
78,480
mph

Mars
54,000
mph

Jupiter
29,000
mph

. . . Rotating speeds are slower.

Venus is the slowest planet in our solar system. It rotates at a speed of only about one mile an hour! The other planets rotate faster. But their rotating speeds are all less than their revolving speeds.

A Comet Is Not a Shooting Star

Comets and shooting stars are flashes of light we
sometimes see in the night sky. But—

Comets have no light of their own . . .

A comet is a ball of ice with bits of rock and metal frozen
inside. Around it is a cloud that can be a million miles across.
A long tail of gas and dust stretches out from the comet's
head. But the comet doesn't produce any light. We see
comets the same way we see planets. They reflect, or bounce
back, light from the sun.

Shooting stars make their own light.

Shooting stars start as solid stone or metal objects in space called meteoroids. Meteoroids become shooting stars, or meteors, when they enter Earth's atmosphere. They come in at a speed of about 25 miles a second! This makes them so hot that they give off light. The heat makes the air around them glow, too. Shooting stars are streaks of light. But they're not comets!

Comets can be seen over several days . . .

Comets follow very long orbits around the sun. From time to time, a comet's orbit brings it close to Earth. Light from the sun makes the comet visible. We can spot it through a telescope or with our eyes. For several days we watch the comet beam across the sky.

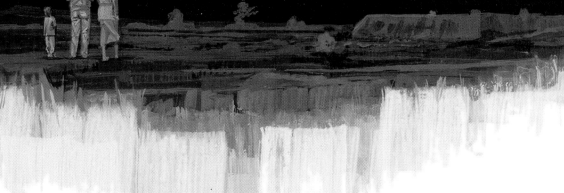

Comets are rarely seen . . .

Some comets go around the sun every few years. It takes others thousands or millions of years to complete their orbits. One of the most famous comets, Halley's Comet, comes near Earth roughly every 77 years. It was here in 1986. The next time will be in the year 2061.

. . . Shooting stars flash for seconds.

Shooting stars, or meteors, start to glow when they are about 65 miles above Earth. By the time they are 40 miles above Earth, they burn out. Their light usually lasts less than a minute.

. . . Shooting stars are seen often.

You can see a meteor or two on almost any clear night. But a few nights a year a shower of meteors glints in the sky. This occurs when Earth's orbit takes it through a swarm of meteoroids. A well-known meteor shower comes in the middle of August. Since the meteors seem to shoot out from the constellation Perseus, we call the shower the Perseid.

Comets never strike Earth . . .

Astronomers have seen about one thousand different comets. But no scientist has ever found traces of a comet that struck Earth.

Once in a great while an enormous meteorite strikes Earth and makes a huge crater. Most meteorites are very small.

. . . Two hundred million meteors reach Earth every day.

Many million meteoroids enter Earth's atmosphere daily. About 200 million become visible meteors. They burn out a few seconds later in Earth's atmosphere. Those that do not burn up completely fall to the ground as meteorites. Meteorites can make holes in the ground called craters.

An Asteroid Is Not a Meteoroid

Asteroids and meteoroids are bodies that move through space. Both travel in orbits around the sun. But—

Asteroids are usually made of stone . . .

Asteroids are like small planets. They contain the same material as Earth. That is, they are mostly made of stone.

. . . Meteoroids are usually made of metal.

A good number of meteoroids are made of metal. The rest are made of stone. The main metal is iron mixed with nickel. Almost all of the meteorites found on Earth contain metal. There are probably lots of stone meteorites on Earth as well. But people think they are ordinary Earth rocks and don't know they are meteorites.

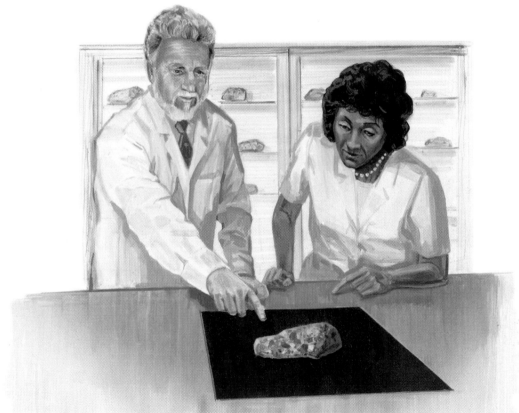

In 1996, astronomers were studying a meteorite that had come to Earth from Mars. In it they found traces of certain chemicals. These chemicals may prove that there was once life on Mars!

Earth

Ceres

Asteroids are measured in miles . . .

The biggest asteroid astronomers have ever seen is named
Ceres. It is about 600 miles across. Compare that with the
size of planet Earth, which is almost 8,000 miles across.
Icarus is the smallest asteroid we know. Its diameter is just
over a half mile.

A huge meteorite that crashed into Greenland is on display in the Museum of Natural History in New York City. This meteorite, called Ahnighito, weighs about half as much as the Hoba West meteorite, which is still in the ground where it fell.

. . . Meteoroids are measured in inches or feet.

Meteoroids are much smaller than asteroids. The largest meteorite is believed to have fallen at Hoba West in Namibia, Africa. It is about nine feet long and weighs about 60 tons. Meteoroids, however, are usually no bigger than a pea or a grain of sand.

Most asteroids are between Mars and Jupiter . . .

Almost all asteroids are in orbit between the planets Mars and Jupiter. Yet from time to time asteroids appear elsewhere. The gravity of the planets sometimes pulls these asteroids into different orbits. And very rarely an asteroid will fall to Earth.

There are about 50,000 known asteroids . . .

Astronomers have photographed as many as 50,000 asteroids. They have numbered and learned the orbits of about 4,000 of these heavenly bodies.

Meteoroids are everywhere in the solar system.

Meteoroids also orbit the sun. But they are scattered all over the solar system. Astronomers think most meteoroids are tiny pieces of metal or stone that have broken off planets, asteroids, or comets.

There are countless meteoroids.

Meteoroids are so small and numerous that they are impossible to count.

A Jet Is Not a Rocket

Both jets and rockets power aircraft through the air at high speeds. But—

Jets need air . . .

Jet engines power airplanes. They burn a mixture of fuel and air inside the engine. In the air is the oxygen that jets need to burn the fuel. The burning fuel builds up gases at tremendous pressure. The gases escape through a nozzle at the back of the engine. This pushes the plane forward.

Jet airliners don't usually fly higher than nine miles. Above that height the air has too little oxygen to power the engines.

. . . Rockets fly without air.

Rocket engines power space shuttles and other spacecraft. They fly up into outer space where there is no air. Rockets carry their own oxygen with them. They usually carry it in the form of liquid oxygen.

Jets burn liquid fuel . . .

Jet engines burn liquid kerosene. The engine draws in air and mixes it with the kerosene. A spark sets the kerosene on fire. The burning fuel forms the hot gases that push the plane forward.

Jets burn fuel slowly . . .

The fuel tanks of a Boeing 747 jet carry fewer than 50,000 gallons of kerosene. But the plane can fly for more than 15 hours with that amount of fuel.

. . . Rockets burn liquid or solid fuels.

Many rocket engines burn liquid hydrogen. The fuel mixes with liquid oxygen in order to burn. An electric spark sets the mixture on fire. The hot gases that result supply thrust for the engine.

Solid rocket engines work differently. They burn a solid material called grain. The grain combines solid fuel with a solid source of oxygen. Workers pack the grain inside the rocket engine. When set on fire, it produces the gases that push the spacecraft forward.

. . . Rockets burn fuel rapidly.

A space shuttle carries two rocket engines. Each holds over 500 tons of solid fuel. The shuttle also carries a tank with 380,000 gallons of liquid hydrogen and 140,000 gallons of liquid oxygen. Yet, the rocket uses up all the fuel in just the first ten minutes of flight! The rest of the mission uses liquid fuel stored inside the shuttle.

A Galaxy Is Not a Constellation

Galaxies and constellations are both groups of stars in outer space. But—

Galaxies may contain over a trillion stars . . .

A galaxy is a huge group of stars held together by gravity. The largest galaxies contain over a trillion stars. The smallest galaxies have fewer than a billion stars. Our sun is in a galaxy that we call the Milky Way. The Milky Way galaxy includes hundreds of billions of stars.

. . . Constellations contain about ten stars.

A constellation is a small group of stars seen from Earth in
a particular part of the night sky. To people who lived long,
long ago, the groups of stars seemed to outline certain pictures. Some looked like animals, such as Leo the lion. Others
looked like legendary gods or heroes, such as Orion the
hunter.

There are about 50 billion galaxies . . .

Astronomers believe that about 50 billion galaxies are spread out over the trillions and trillions of miles of space. Photographs taken through telescopes show about one million galaxies.

. . . There are only 88 constellations.

Astronomers have divided the night sky into 88 constellations. The constellations form a kind of map in the sky. They give people on Earth a good way to locate particular stars, planets, comets, meteors, and other objects in space. Do you want to find the North Star? Look in the constellation Ursa Minor (also known as the Little Dipper).

From earliest times, sailors have used the constellations to help keep their boats on course during the night.

The stars in galaxies are close to one another . . .

The billions of stars in a galaxy are all clustered together.
They form two main galaxy shapes—spiral and elliptical. A
spiral galaxy, such as like the Milky Way, has masses of stars
crowded in the center. The rest of the stars form curved arms
coming out from the middle. The whole galaxy looks like a
giant pinwheel. Elliptical galaxies range in shape from round
globes to flat circles or ovals.

Spiral galaxy

The stars in constellations are far apart.

The stars are all in the Milky Way galaxy. But they are not all the same distance from Earth. Some stars are closer to Earth; some are much farther away. The stars in a constellation are usually billions and billions of miles apart.

Elliptical galaxy

Astrology Is Not Astronomy

Both astrology and astronomy study the stars and planets. But—

Astrology studies the effects of the stars and planets . . .

Many people believe that the stars and planets influence their lives and can help to forecast the future. They try to understand how the heavenly bodies affect everyday events. This study is called astrology.

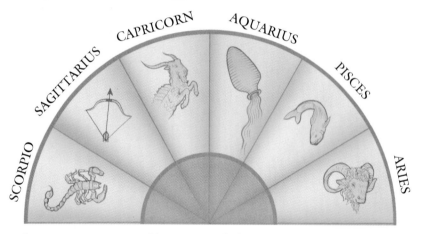

Astrologers use zodiacs and horoscopes . . .

Astrologers tell people's fortunes with a star diagram, called a zodiac. The zodiac is divided into twelve signs named for the constellations. Based on a person's birthday, astrologers draw, or "cast," a horoscope. A simple horoscope describes a person's character. For example, someone born under the sign of Leo (July 23 to August 22) is believed to be sunny and cheerful.

. . . Astronomy studies the stars and planets.

Astronomy is a science that investigates the stars, planets, and other objects in space. The scientists seek answers to many questions. Where has the object been and where is it going? How fast is it moving? What is it made of? Why and how is it changing? Are there new objects to be found?

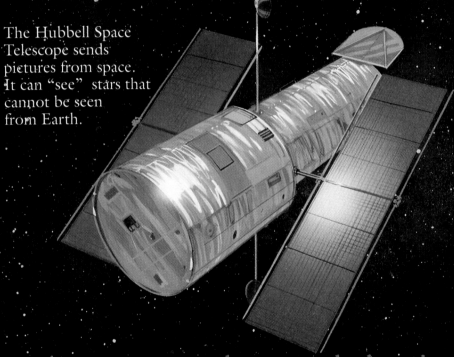

The Hubbell Space Telescope sends pictures from space. It can "see" stars that cannot be seen from Earth.

. . . Astronomers use telescopes and other scientific instruments.

Astronomers use the most modern tools in their studies: telescopes to get a better look at objects in space; radio telescopes to pick up natural radio signals from distant stars; cameras to photograph every area of the sky; and instruments that they land on the moon and planets to collect samples and make measurements.

Astrology is not a real science . . .

Astrology started thousands of years ago. The ancient peoples learned a lot about the stars and planets by looking up at the heavens. Early on they decided that the stars or planets influence people and events on Earth. Yet no one has ever been able to prove this is so. Nonetheless, astrologers continue to follow the old beliefs.

. . . Astronomy is a true science.

Astronomy depends on scientists checking one another's discoveries and experiments. They test the findings and look for proofs. Suppose an astronomer finds a new comet. Others must be able to see it, too. They must be sure no one has seen it before. Only then can the astronomer give it a name.

Some Final Mix-ups

You've just read some of the best-known space and sky mix-ups. Here are a few more quickies.

The Milky Way Is Not a Candy Bar

To most of us, Milky Way is a candy bar made with milk chocolate. But to astronomers, the Milky Way is our home galaxy. It is a huge spiral galaxy, with hundreds of billions of stars. The Milky Way galaxy also includes the sun, Earth, and the other planets of the solar system.

Do you wonder how the galaxy got its name? Go outdoors on the next dark, clear night and look up. You'll see a white band across the sky. It consists of millions of stars. Someone thought it looked like a spilled pail of milk. They called it the Milky Way. Then astronomers named the whole galaxy the Milky Way. And later, the candy maker called the chocolate bar Milky Way.

The Big Bang Is Not a Loud Noise

What is the loudest noise you can imagine? That's nothing compared to what astronomers call the big bang. The big bang was an explosion that scientists believe occurred 13 billion years ago. Once, everything in the universe was squeezed together into a very small, very heavy fireball. Then—BOOM!!!—this fireball exploded. Nearly all astronomers believe this explosion started the universe.

The Evening Star Is Not a Star

For ages, people have noticed a bright object in the evening sky. They call it the Evening Star. But it is not a star at all. It is the planet Venus! Venus is the third brightest object in the sky. Only the sun and moon are brighter. Venus can be seen shining brightly right after sunset. And it rises before the sun in the morning.